Ratios and Percents

Harcourt Achieve

Rigby • Saxon • Steck-Vaughn

www.HarcourtAchieve.com

1.800.531.5015

Acknowledgments

Editorial Director	Ellen Northcutt
Supervising Editor	Pamela Sears
Senior Editor	Kathy Immel
Associate Design Director	Joyce Spicer
Design Team	Jim Cauthron
	Joan Cunningham
Photo Researcher	Stephanie Arsenault
Cover Art	©Janet Parke
Photography Credits	p. 6 ©Richard Cummins/CORBIS;
	p. 28 ©Jeff Greenberg/AGE Fotostock;
	p. 58 Courtesy Sam Dudgeon/HRW Studio

ISBN 1-4190-0369-0

5 6 7 8 9 10 862 11 10 09 08

Contents

To the Student

Building a solid foundation in math is your key to success in school and in the future. Working with the *Top Line Math* books will help you to develop the basic math skills that you use every day. As you build on math skills that you already know and learn new math skills, you will see how much math connects to real life.

When you read the Overviews in this *Top Line Math* book, read You Know and You Will Learn. As you focus on new math skills, consider how they connect to what you already know.

Pretest and Post Test

Take the Pretest at the beginning of this book. Your results on the Pretest will show you which math skills you already know and which ones you need to develop.

When you have finished working in this book, take the Post Test. Your results on the Post Test will show you how much you have learned.

Practice

Practice pages allow you to practice the skills you have learned in the lesson. You will solve both computation problems and word problems.

Unit Reviews

Unit Reviews let you see how well you have learned the skills and concepts presented in each unit.

Test–Taking Strategy

Every test-taking strategy shows you various tools you can use when taking tests.

Glossary

Each lesson has **key words** that are important to know. Turn to the glossary at the end of the book to learn the meaning of new words. Use the definitions and examples to strengthen your understanding of math terms.

Setting Goals

A goal is something you aim for, something you want to achieve. It is important to set goals throughout your life so you can plan realistic ways to get what you want.

Successful people in all fields set goals. Think about your own goals.

- Where do you see yourself after high school?
- What do you want to be doing 10 years from now?
- What steps do you need to take to get to your goals?

Goal setting is a step-by-step process. To start this process, you need to think about what you want and how you will get it. Setting a long-term goal is a way to plan for the future. A short-term goal is one of the steps you take to achieve your long-term goal.

What is your long-term goal for using this book about ratios and percents? You may want to improve your test scores or you may want to become better at math so you can become a master chef.

Write your long-term goal for learning math.

_____

_____

Think about how you already use ratios and percents. Then, set some short-term goals for what you would like to learn in this book. These short-term goals will help you to reach your long-term goal.

I use ratios and percents in my everyday life to

☐ figure out a sale discount.

☐ know how much to tip for a restaurant meal.

☐ find out how many miles per gallon my car gets.

☐ _____

My short-term goals for using this book are

_____

_____

Pretest

Take this Pretest before you begin this book. Do not worry if you cannot easily answer all the questions. The Pretest will help you determine which skills you are already strong in and which skills you need to practice.

Use the figures below to answer numbers 1 and 2. Be sure your answer is in simplest form.

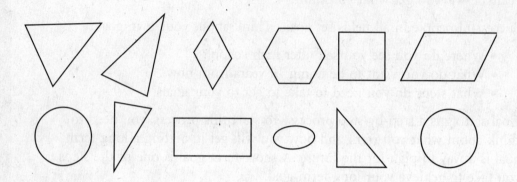

1. What is the ratio of circles to triangles?

2. What is the ratio of triangles to total figures?

Write each rate in simplest form.

3. 12 pages in 3 minutes

4. 80 kilometers in 4 hours

Solve.

5. Roy bought 6 cans of juice for $1.32. What is the price per can?

6. A 3-pound melon sells for $2.10. What is the price per pound?

Write = or ≠ in the box.

7. $\frac{3}{8} \,\square\, \frac{6}{10}$

8. $\frac{4}{9} \,\square\, \frac{12}{27}$

Solve for *n*.

9. $\frac{6}{n} = \frac{9}{6}$

10. $\frac{n}{20} = \frac{45}{15}$

Solve.

11. Two out of every 9 students were accepted into the marching band. If 225 students applied, how many were accepted?

12. Ramon is paid by the hour. During one 35-hour week he earned $420. What is Ramon's hourly pay?

Write each decimal or fraction as a percent.

13. 0.065

14. $\frac{7}{8}$

Write each percent as a fraction in simplest form.

15. 32%

16. 125%

Solve.

17. Find 22% of 60.

18. What percent of 40 is 24?

19. 1.2 is 40% percent of what number?

20. 22 is what percent of 88?

21. Meg sold 75% of her collection of DVDs. She sold 30 DVDs. How many were in her collection?

22. At *Gene's Jeans Store,* all items go on sale for 15% off if they have not sold after being in the store for one week. If a pair of jeans is originally priced at $40, how much do they cost 10 days later?

Find the interest.

23. $600 deposited for 2 years at annual rate of 4% simple interest

24. $4,000 deposited for 9 months at 5.5% simple interest

Find the balance in the account.

25. Principal: $250; compound interest rate: 5%; compounded semi-annually; time: 1 year

Ratio and Proportion

Real-Life Matters

Two DVD stores at the mall want your business. At Movie Time you can rent four DVDs for $15. DVD World rents DVDs for $4.50 each.

When you rent DVDs, you want the price to be as low as possible. How can you figure out which company has the lowest price? Compare the price of each DVD. For Movie Time, divide the total price, $15, by the number of DVDs, 4. Each DVD is $3.75. As long as you rent four DVDs at a time, Movie Time is the better deal.

You can also use a **ratio** to find the answer. A ratio compares two numbers. The fraction $\frac{15}{4}$ is a specific ratio. It compares the total price to the number of DVDs.

A **proportion** means that two ratios are equal.
$$\frac{15}{4} = \frac{3.75}{1}$$
Proportions can help you find a missing piece of information.

Real-Life Application

Another DVD rental company has a special offer. You can rent an unlimited number of DVDs in one month for just $21.00. How much would each DVD cost if you rented 7 DVDs in one month?

_____

How would the cost change if you rented 14 DVDs in one month?

_____

Imagine that the lowest price you found was $3.00 for each DVD rental. You still have only $21.00 to spend each month. How many DVDs could you rent each month with this plan?

_____

Tell which DVD rental plan you would use and explain why.

_____

_____

Overview • Lessons 1-3

Ratios and Rates

You have worked with fractions and equivalent, or equal, fractions. You have simplified fractions using a greatest common factor (GCF). Now you are ready to work with ratios.

Look at the six-slice pie at the right.

Two of the slices are blueberry. Four of them are apple.

$$\frac{\text{Part}}{\text{Whole}} = \frac{2}{6} = \frac{1}{3}$$

A ratio compares two quantities. The ratio of blueberry slices to all slices is $\frac{1}{3}$ in simplest form.

Ratios can be written in 3 ways.

fraction form	with a colon	in words
$\frac{1}{3}$	1 : 3	1 to 3

YOU KNOW

- That fractions show parts of a whole

- That equivalent fractions name the same quantity

- How to write a fraction in its simplest form by using the greatest common factor (GCF)

YOU WILL LEARN

- That ratios compare two quantities

- How to reduce ratios to their simplest forms

- That rates and unit rates are special kinds of ratios

Remember the BASICS

For each fraction given, write two equivalent fractions.

FRACTION	EQUIVALENT FRACTION	EQUIVALENT FRACTION
$\frac{8}{10}$	$= \frac{4}{5}$	$= \frac{16}{20}$
$\frac{3}{7}$	$=$	$=$
$\frac{5}{12}$	$=$	$=$
$\frac{1}{4}$	$=$	$=$
$\frac{12}{18}$	$=$	$=$
$\frac{3}{8}$	$=$	$=$

LESSON ❶ Ratios

You probably have heard people say things like *The ratio of boys to girls in the class is 12 to 11.* or *On a piano, the ratio of black keys to white keys is 5 to 7.*

A **ratio** compares two amounts or numbers. Like fractions, ratios must be written in *simplest form*.

Ratios can be written as

a fraction
$$\frac{1}{2}$$

with a colon
$$1 : 2$$

in words
1 to 2

Example

This basketball team has 9 players.

Look at the uniforms. Write a ratio comparing the number of uniforms that have odd numbers to the number of uniforms that have even numbers.

STEP 1   Identify the numbers that you need to compare.

odd numbers	even numbers
6 uniforms	3 uniforms

STEP 2   Write a ratio.
odd to even 6 to 3 or $\frac{6}{3}$

STEP 3   Write the ratio in simplest form.
Reduce $\frac{6}{3}$ to simplest form by dividing. Use their GCF.
$$\frac{6}{3} \div \frac{3}{3} = \frac{2}{1}$$

In simplest form, the ratio is
2 to 1, 2 : 1, or $\frac{2}{1}$.

Finding the GCF of 6 and 3:

• Factors of 6 are 1, 2, ③, 6

• Factors of 3 are 1, ③

3 is the GCF of 6 and 3

ON YOUR OWN

There are 24 students in the school musical. Ten of the students are seniors. What is the ratio of students who are seniors to students who are *not* seniors?

Practice

Building Skills

Write each ratio in three ways. Reduce to simplest form.

There are 18 students on the school bus. There are 5 seniors, 2 juniors, 6 sophomores, and 5 freshmen.

1. What is the ratio of juniors to freshmen?

$2 : 5$, 2 to 5, or $\dfrac{2}{5}$

2. What is the ratio of juniors to seniors?

3. What is the ratio of sophomores to seniors?

4. What is the ratio of sophomores to all bus riders?

Use the grouping of letters to answer questions 5–8. Reduce the ratio to simplest form.

$$\text{C A C A C B C}$$
$$\text{A A B C B C A}$$

5. What is the ratio of As to Bs?

6. What is the ratio of As to Cs?

7. What is the ratio of Bs to Cs?

8. What is the ratio of Cs to As *and* Bs?

Problem Solving

Write a ratio.

9. Write a ratio to compare the number of letters in the word *Picasso* with the number of letters in the word *Shakespeare*.

$7 : 11$ or $\dfrac{7}{11}$

10. Sarah swims 35 laps. Kevin swims 25 laps. Write a ratio comparing the number of laps that Kevin swims to the number of laps that Sarah swims.

11. Ethan and Ben played against each other in a trivia game. Ethan scored 8 points and Ben scored 12 points. Write the ratio, in simplest form, that compares their scores.

12. In a school spirit contest, Pat's team of 11 people had 7 of the winning costumes. Write a ratio that compares the number of winning costumes to the total number of people on the team.

LESSON 2 Rates

You have learned about ratios. Now you are ready to learn about a special kind of ratio called a rate. A **rate** is a ratio that compares two amounts measured in *different* kinds of units. Here are examples:

250 *miles* in 4 *hours*	Inez drove at a rate of 250 miles in 4 hours.
200 *sit-ups* in 30 *minutes*	Alex can do 200 sit-ups in 30 minutes.
200 *dollars* for 1 *day*	Lee charges clients $200 for one day of work.

You use and see rates every day. When you go shopping, you might see a sign similar to the one above.

Example

Use the sale sign above. Write the sale price for CDs as a rate. Express the rate in simplest form.

STEP 1 Write the numbers you are comparing as a fraction.

The rate is $\dfrac{24 \text{ dollars}}{3 \text{ CDs}}$.

STEP 2 Express the rate in simplest form.
Divide the numerator and denominator by their GCF, 3.

$$= \frac{24 \text{ dollars} \div 3}{3 \text{ CDs} \div 3}$$

$$= \frac{8 \text{ dollars}}{1 \text{ CD}}$$

CDs are selling at the rate of $8 per CD.

ON YOUR OWN

Marcus can flip a coin 140 times in 4 minutes. At what rate does he flip a coin?

Practice

To simplify, find the GCF.

Building Skills

Write each rate in simplest form.

1. 10 miles in 6 hours

$$\frac{10 \text{ miles} \div 2}{6 \text{ hours} \div 2} = \frac{5 \text{ miles}}{3 \text{ hours}}$$

2. 20 dollars for 6 books

3. 9 free throws in 24 attempts

4. 50 liters in 4 minutes

5. $32 earned in 4 hours

6. 5 tickets for $80

7. 6 cups of flour for 4 eggs

8. $300 for 4 tires

9. 10 laps in 5 minutes

Problem Solving

Write each rate in simplest form.

10. Abdul drove 80 miles in 2 hours.

$$\frac{80 \text{ miles}}{2 \text{ hours}} = \frac{40 \text{ miles}}{1 \text{hour}}$$

11. In 4 hours, Carmen used 10 rolls of film.

12. Jerome swims 15 laps in 20 minutes.

13. The Tanaka family spent $105 for a 14-day travel pass.

14. Maria's dog chased 30 squirrels in 4 hours.

15. Olivia used 30 gallons of gas on a 510-mile road trip.

You have learned that a rate is a ratio comparing different kinds of units. You also know that rates can be simplified like fractions. Now you will learn about a very useful kind of rate called a *unit rate*.

A **unit rate** is the rate for *one* unit of a quantity. Here are some examples:

$$\frac{45 \text{ miles}}{\text{hour}} \qquad \frac{65 \text{ words}}{\text{minute}} \qquad \frac{25 \text{ students}}{\text{teacher}}$$

The denominator for any unit rate is 1—as in *1* hour, *1* minute, or *1* teacher.

A unit rate that tells the price per unit is called a **unit price.**

$$\frac{\$3.00}{\text{box}} \qquad \frac{\$0.25}{\text{can}} \qquad \frac{\$2.79}{\text{fluid ounce}}$$

9 servings = 72 grams of fiber

1 serving = ? grams of fiber

When you read nutrition facts on food packages, you are reading unit rates.

Example

A box of cereal contains 9 servings and a total of 72 grams of fiber. How many grams of fiber are in one serving?
(One serving is 1 unit.)

STEP 1 Write the numbers as a fraction.

$$\frac{72 \text{ grams}}{9 \text{ servings}}$$

STEP 2 Divide.

$$\frac{72 \text{ grams}}{9 \text{ servings}} = \frac{8 \text{ grams}}{1 \text{ serving}}$$

There are 8 grams of fiber in one serving.

ON YOUR OWN

Jamal drove 66 miles in $2\frac{1}{2}$ hours. How many *miles per hour* did he drive?

Practice

Building Skills

Write the unit rate or unit price.

1. 60 miles in 4 hours

$$\frac{60\text{ miles}}{4\text{ hours}} \div \frac{4}{4} = \frac{15\text{ miles}}{1\text{ hour}}$$

The unit rate is 15 miles per hour.

2. $45 for 5 hours

3. 200 words in 4 minutes

4. 88 miles in 2 hours

5. 6 cans of juice for $1.80

6. 36 grams of fat in 6 servings

7. 3,000 meters in 10 minutes

8. 144 miles on 6 gallons

9. 90 pages in 180 minutes

Problem Solving

Write the unit rate in simplest form.

10. Twelve small bottles of juice sell for $4.80.

$$\frac{\$4.80}{12\text{ bottles}} = \$.40/\text{bottle}$$

11. Barak reads 60 pages in 30 minutes.

12. Rob can type 500 words in 10 minutes.

13. A pizza that costs $9 has 6 slices.

14. The Ramos family pays $350 for 4 rooms at an inn.

15. Five-pound watermelons are on sale for $4 each. Find the price per pound.

TEST–TAKING STRATEGY

Use Logical Reasoning

You can use a Venn diagram to answer test questions about ratios.

Example

The World Language Club has 15 students. Nine students speak French, and 6 speak Spanish. Four students speak both languages. What is the ratio of students who speak only French to students who speak only Spanish?

STEP 1 Draw and label a Venn diagram.

STEP 2 Fill in the Venn diagram.
Place the number of students who speak both French and Spanish where the two circles overlap.
Nine students speak French. Of these students, 4 also speak Spanish. The number who speak only French is 9 – 4, or 5. Write 5 in the oval labeled French.
Six students speak Spanish. Of these students, 4 also speak French. So, 6 – 4, or 2 students speak Spanish only. Write 2 in the oval labeled Spanish.

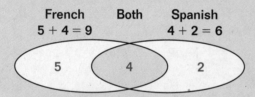

STEP 3 Write a ratio to compare.

| students who speak only French | → | 5 |
| students who speak only Spanish | → | 2 |

The ratio is 5 to 2.

TRY IT OUT

There are 13 customers in a diner. The waitress serves soup to 6 customers and salad to 7 customers. She serves both soup and salad to 3 of those customers. What is the ratio of customers who had both soup and salad to customers who had only salad?

Circle the correct answer.

A. 3 to 3   **B.** 3 to 7   **C.** 4 to 3   **D.** 3 to 4

Option D is correct. Three customers had both soup and salad. Of the 7 customers who had salad, 7 – 3, or 4, customers had only salad.

Overview • Lessons 4-5

Proportions

You have worked with ratios, rates, and unit rates. Now you are ready to work with proportions. You will also learn what cross products are and how to use them.

Look at this price list from a bagel shop.

Food	Price
bagels	$6 for 1 dozen
juice	$2 per quart
sweet rolls	$4 for 10 rolls

What if you want to buy 3 bagels, 6 bagels, or even 20 bagels? What if you want to buy 3 quarts of juice or 40 rolls? You could use a proportion to find the answers. A **proportion** is a statement that says 2 ratios are equal. In the next lesson, you will to learn more about ratios and proportions.

CENTRAL SQUARE BAKERY

YOU KNOW

- That ratios are comparisons of two amounts
- That equivalent ratios compare the same amounts
- That an equation is a statement that says two amounts are equal

YOU WILL LEARN

- How to set up a proportion
- How to use cross products

Remember the BASICS

For each ratio, write an equivalent ratio in simplest form.

RATIO	RATIO IN SIMPLEST FORM	RATIO	RATIO IN SIMPLEST FORM
4 : 6	2 : 3	14 to 28	
$\frac{3}{9}$		$\frac{12}{20}$	
5 to 20		10 : 24	

LESSON 4 Proportions

You know that ratios make comparisons. Two ratios that make the same comparison are called equivalent ratios.

A statement that shows two ratios as equal is called a **proportion**.

To check to see if the ratios are equal, **cross multiply.** If the **cross products** are equal, they form a proportion.

$$\frac{1}{3} = \frac{2}{6} \qquad 3 \times 2 = 6$$
$$1 \times 6 = 6$$

Because $6 = 6$ the ratios are a proportion.

> **equivalent**—when two things are equal

$$\frac{2 \text{ basketballs}}{6 \text{ basketballs}} = \frac{1 \text{ basketball}}{3 \text{ basketballs}}$$

Equivalent ratios are proportions.

Example

On a test, Suki got 6 answers right out of 9. Jim got 8 answers right out of 10. Are the students' scores proportional?

STEP 1 Set up the two ratios. Be sure that the numbers in the ratios are set up in correct order.

Suki	Jim
$\frac{6}{9}$	$\frac{8}{10}$

STEP 2 Find the cross products.

$$\frac{6}{9} \times \frac{8}{10}$$

$$6 \times 10 = 60$$
$$9 \times 8 = 72$$

STEP 3 Compare the cross products.

$60 \neq 72$, so the ratios are *not* a proportion. Suki and Jim's scores are <u>not</u> proportional.

ON YOUR OWN

This summer 8 out of 12 people took a vacation. Last summer 3 out of 4 people took a vacation. Are these ratios proportional?

Practice

Building Skills

Write = or ≠ between the ratios.

1. $2 : 3$ = $12 : 18$

$2 \times 18 = 3 \times 12$
$36 = 36$

2. $\dfrac{3}{8}$ $\dfrac{6}{18}$

3. $\dfrac{2}{5}$ $\dfrac{8}{20}$

4. $6 : 8$ $12 : 16$

5. $4 : 9$ $12 : 26$

6. $\dfrac{3}{7}$ $\dfrac{14}{6}$

7. $\dfrac{7}{2}$ $\dfrac{21}{6}$

8. $9 : 5$ $27 : 9$

9. $\dfrac{2}{8}$ $\dfrac{20}{80}$

Problem Solving

Use proportions to solve these problems.

10. Jim gets paid $40 for 4 hours of work. Carmela gets paid $60 for 6 hours of work. Do Jim and Carmela get paid at the same rate?

$\dfrac{40}{4}$? $\dfrac{60}{6}$; $(4 \times 60) = (40 \times 6)$
$240 = 240$
Yes, they get paid at the same rate.

11. Anna saves $3 for every $10 she earns. Patrick saves $5 for every $20 he earns. Do the two save money at the same rate?

12. Henry completed 6 of the 15 passes he attempted. Giovanni completed 9 of his 21 passes. Did the two quarterbacks complete passes at the same rate?

13. Jackie can type 50 words in a minute. Her brother can type 200 words in 4 minutes. Are their typing speeds the same?

14. Keonta can walk half a mile in ten minutes. Abigail walks one mile in 25 minutes. Do Keonta and Abigail walk at the same rate?

15. Emily answered 8 of 10 questions correctly on a test. On a different test, Yuki answered 15 of 20 questions correctly. Did Emily and Yuki have the same ratio of correct answers?

You know that you can use cross products to find whether two ratios form a proportion. You can also use cross products to find a missing number in a proportion.

It doesn't matter how you set up the ratios as long as the same categories are on top and the same categories are on the bottom.

Example

Read the clipping. If Keisha keeps getting hits at this same rate, how many hits will she get in 60 at-bats?

> ### Teen Slugger Leads the Way
>
> Keisha Jones is off to a big start this season with 4 hits in her first 12 at-bats. Her 9th inning round-tripper gave the Tigers their third straight victory.

STEP 1 Set up a proportion.
You do not know how many hits Keisha got in 60 at-bats. Use a letter, such as n, to substitute for the unknown number.

$$\frac{\text{hits}}{\text{at-bats}} \rightarrow \frac{4}{12} = \frac{n}{60}$$

STEP 2 Cross multiply.

$$\frac{4}{12} \bowtie \frac{n}{60}$$

$$12 \times n = 4 \times 60$$
$$12n = 240$$

STEP 3 Solve for n.
Divide both sides by 12 because n is next to 12.
$$12n = 240$$
$$\frac{12n}{12} = \frac{240}{12}$$
$$n = 20$$
$$\frac{4}{12} = \frac{20}{60}$$

Keisha would get 20 hits in 60 at-bats.

ON YOUR OWN

One photo is 6 inches long and 4 inches wide. You can enlarge the photo so that it will be 18 inches long. How wide will the photo be?

Practice

Divide both sides by the number next to *n*.

Building Skills

Solve each proportion.

1. $\dfrac{3}{4} = \dfrac{n}{12}$

$3 \times 12 = 4 \times n$
$36 = 4n$
$\dfrac{36}{4} = \dfrac{4n}{4}, 9 = n$
$\dfrac{3}{4} = \dfrac{9}{12}$

2. $\dfrac{4}{n} = \dfrac{6}{9}$

3. $\dfrac{8}{16} = \dfrac{n}{4}$

4. $\dfrac{n}{30} = \dfrac{5}{6}$

5. $\dfrac{18}{30} = \dfrac{n}{10}$

6. $\dfrac{40}{n} = \dfrac{8}{5}$

7. $\dfrac{5}{25} = \dfrac{4}{n}$

8. $\dfrac{3}{8} = \dfrac{21}{n}$

9. $\dfrac{n}{20} = \dfrac{11}{4}$

Problem Solving

Use proportions to solve these problems.

10. LaToya gets paid by the hour. During a 20-hour week, LaToya earns $120. If she works only 15 hours, how much does she earn?

$(120 \times 15) = (20 \times n)$
$1,800 = 20n$
$90 = n$

11. Joe is a photographer. For every 15 rolls of film he shoots, 10 are black and white. If Joe uses 57 rolls of film, how many rolls are in black and white?

12. Luisa swims 35 laps in 25 minutes. How many laps will she swim in 10 minutes?

13. Darnell walks 140 minutes in 4 days. At this rate how many minutes will he walk in 6 days?

14. Dan scored 80 points in 5 basketball games. At this rate, how many points do you expect him to score in 20 games?

15. Jay buys 60 square feet of tile for $324. Later, he buys another 20 square feet of tile. How much does the extra tile cost?

TEST–TAKING STRATEGY

Write Proportions to Solve Word Problems.

Sometimes it is hard to begin to solve a word problem. If the problems compare categories or numbers, you can begin by writing a proportion. Be sure to reduce each ratio to make multiplication easier.

Example

A survey shows that 27 out of 63 ninth-grade students have part-time jobs. There are 56 tenth-grade students. Based on the ratio for ninth-grade students, how many tenth-grade students have part-time jobs?

STEP 1 Write a ratio to show what you are comparing.

$$\frac{\text{9th-grade students with part-time jobs}}{\text{total number of 9th grade students}} \quad \frac{27}{63} = \frac{3}{7}$$

STEP 2 Write another ratio. Compare tenth-grade students with part-time jobs to the total number of tenth-grade students.

$$\frac{\text{10th-grade students who have part-time jobs}}{\text{total number of 10th-grade students}} = \frac{n}{56}$$

You don't know the number of tenth-grade students who have jobs, so let n stand for the missing number.

STEP 3 Write a proportion and solve.

There are 24 tenth-grade students with part-time jobs.

$$\frac{3}{7} = \frac{n}{56}$$
$$7n = 3 \times 56$$
$$7n = 168$$
$$\frac{7n}{7} = \frac{168}{7} = 24$$

TRY IT OUT

An artist mixes 10 ounces of red paint with 15 ounces of blue paint to get purple. If she mixes 8 ounces of red paint, how many ounces of blue paint will she need?
Circle the correct answer.

A. 10   B. 15   C. 12   D. 5.3

Option C is correct.
$$\frac{\text{red}}{\text{blue}} = \frac{10}{15} = \frac{8}{n} \qquad 10n = 15 \times 8 \qquad \frac{10n}{10} = \frac{120}{10} \qquad n = 12$$

Overview • Lessons 6–7

More on Proportions

You know that the cross-products of a proportion are equal. You also know how to use the cross-products to find a missing term in the proportion.

You can use proportions to solve everyday problems. This is called *proportional reasoning*. Problems about sports, nutrition, wages, shopping, and even map reading can be solved using proportional reasoning.

Look at the map on the right.

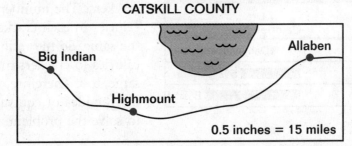

CATSKILL COUNTY

Big Indian

Allaben

Highmount

0.5 inches = 15 miles

By applying proportional reasoning, you can figure out how far Highmount is from Allaben. According to the map scale, 0.5 inch = 15 miles. Highmount measures about 2 inches from Allaben. So you can write:

$$\frac{0.5 \text{ inches}}{15 \text{ miles}} = \frac{2 \text{ inches}}{n \text{ miles}}$$

Find the cross-products. Then solve for n: $0.5 \times n = 15 \times 2$, $0.5n = 30$, $n = 60$

Highmount is about 60 miles from Allaben.

In the lesson that follows, you will learn more about writing proportions to solve everyday kinds of problems.

YOU KNOW

- How to set up ratios and proportions

- How to cross-multiply

- How to solve for n in a proportion

YOU WILL LEARN

- How to write proportions for everyday situations

- How to use equivalent ratios and proportional reasoning to solve problems

Remember the BASICS

Solve each proportion. If you need to review, turn to page 16.

$\frac{3}{4} = \frac{n}{12}$	$\frac{30}{18} = \frac{10}{n}$	$\frac{3}{8} = \frac{n}{40}$
$3 \times 12 = 4 \times n$		
$4n = 36; \ n = 9$		
So, $\frac{3}{4} = \frac{9}{12}$		

Up until now, you have solved proportions by finding cross-products. The numbers used in proportions are called **terms**. Each time, three of the four terms, of the proportion were already written. You could then solve for the missing term.

Sometimes, you will have to write the proportion yourself before you can solve. Look at the nutrition facts below.

Nutrition Facts	
Serving Size 2 crackers (13g)	
Servings Per Container About 20	
Amount Per Serving	
Calories 70	Calories from Fat 30
	%Daily Value*
Total Fat 3g	5%
Saturated Fat 1.5g	8%

You just ate seven crackers. How can you find the total number of calories in seven crackers? The number of calories in each cracker stays the same. So the ratio of calories to crackers must be the same, too. Therefore, you can use the idea of equivalent ratios to solve the problem.

Example

Look at the nutrition facts above. How many calories are in 7 crackers?

STEP 1 Identify the information you have.
- A serving size is two crackers.
- There are 70 calories in one serving.
- You ate seven crackers.

STEP 2 Write a proportion to show the comparisons.
One serving is two crackers. There are 70 calories in two crackers. Use the letter n to stand for the unknown number of calories in 7 crackers.

$$\frac{70 \text{ calories}}{2 \text{ crackers}} = \frac{n \text{ calories}}{7 \text{ crackers}} \leftarrow \text{Equivalent ratios that form a proportion must compare the } same \text{ units in the } same \text{ order.}$$

STEP 3 Solve for n.

$$\frac{70}{2} = \frac{n}{7}$$
$$70 \times 7 = 2 \times n$$
$$490 = 2n$$
$$245 = n$$

There are 245 calories in 7 crackers.

ON YOUR OWN

Julio can type 90 words in 2 minutes. He needs to take a 5-minute typing test in order to get a job. If Julio types at his usual rate, how many words will he type on this test?

Practice

Building Skills

Set up a proportion to solve each problem.

1. You work 3 hours every 2 days. How many hours do you work in 6 days?

$$\frac{3}{2} = \frac{n}{6}, (3 \times 6) = (2 \times n)$$
$$18 = 2n, n = 9$$

2. You read 42 pages in 3 hours. How many hours will it take you to read 147 pages?

3. It takes you 20 minutes to outline 5 pages in your history book. How much time will it take you to outline a 30-page chapter?

4. There were 7 field goals made in 14 attempts. How many goals should be made in 8 attempts?

5. You attend club meetings 18 days per month. How many meetings do you attend in 9 months?

6. A bus driver picks up 40 people in 5 hours. How many people does she pick up in 40 hours?

7. You can type 171 words in 3 hours. How many words do you type per hour?

8. Two out of every 7 students who apply to work in the library get a job. If 30 students have a library job, how many students applied?

Problem Solving

Write a proportion to solve each problem.

9. Eric earns $390 during a 30-hour week. How much does he earn per hour?

$$\frac{\$390}{30 \text{ hours}} = \frac{n}{1 \text{ hour}}$$
$$(390 \times 1) = (30 \times n), 390 = 30n, \$13 = n$$

10. There are 360 calories in 6 servings. How many calories are in a single serving?

11. Kim runs 8 laps in 20 minutes. At that rate, how many laps could he run in 60 minutes?

12. Lisa made 8 cell phone calls in 12 minutes. At that rate, how many calls will she make in 30 minutes?

13. You can finish 36 math problems in one hour. How many problems would you finish in 30 minutes?

14. A recipe for carrot salad makes 12 servings. The recipe calls for 2 cups of grated carrots. You only have half a cup. How many servings can you make?

LESSON 7 Problem Solving Using Proportions

You know that you can use proportions to solve everyday problems. When you write a proportion, think about the following:

- All rates should stay the same.

- Make sure that both ratios compare the same units in the same order.

Look at the grocery-store ad at the right. If 6 limes cost $0.90, then twice as many limes cost twice as much. This proportion shows that the price for each lime is the same.

$$\frac{6 \text{ limes}}{\$0.90} = \frac{12 \text{ limes}}{\$1.80}$$

TODAY ONLY

Fruit Sale!

3 pints of blueberries	$5.00
2 honeydew melons	$5.00
1 dozen oranges	$3.00
6 limes	$0.90

Example

Look at the ad above. You are making blueberry muffins. You have $15 to buy blueberries. How many pints of blueberries can you buy?

STEP 1 Identify the information you have.
- 3 pints of blueberries for $5
- $15 to spend

STEP 2 Write a proportion to show the comparisons.
Compare the *same* units in the *same* order. One way is to compare blueberry pints for $5 with blueberry pints for $15.

$$\frac{3 \text{ pints}}{\$5} = \frac{n \text{ pints}}{\$15}$$

STEP 3 Solve the proportion.

$$\frac{3}{\$5} = \frac{n}{\$15}$$

$$\frac{45}{5} = \frac{5n}{5} \leftarrow \text{Divide both sides by 5 to find } n.$$

$$n = 9$$

For $15, you can buy 9 pints of blueberries.

ON YOUR OWN

Look at the ad again. You need to buy some honeydew melons. How much will 5 melons cost?

Practice

Problem Solving

Write a proportion to solve each problem.

1. If 3 onions weigh 1 pound, how much do 12 onions weigh?

$$\frac{3}{1} = \frac{12}{n} \quad \begin{array}{l}\leftarrow \text{onions} \\ \leftarrow \text{pounds}\end{array}$$

$3 \times n = 1 \times 12$

$3n = 12$

$n = 4$

Twelve onions weigh 4 pounds.

2. If 5 tropical fish cost $6, how much will 10 tropical fish cost?

3. You buy a package of pens for $4.80. There are 12 pens in the package. How much would 10 pens cost?

4. Roses are on sale 6 for $10. How many roses could you buy for $15?

5. You guess that you can bike 35 miles in 2 hours. At that rate, how far could you bike in 6 hours?

6. A recipe for applesauce serves 8 people. You need three-quarters of a cup of water. Suppose you are making the recipe for 12 people. How much water will you need?

7. You volunteer to make calls for your favorite charity. You can make 24 calls in 2 hours. At that rate, how many calls can you make in half an hour?

8. One dozen bananas weighs three pounds. What do 2 bananas weigh?

9. The school band plays for 20 minutes at a pep rally. They play 10 songs. If all the songs are the same length, how many songs do they play in 5 minutes?

10. You reach into a large bag of marbles and pull out a handful of 20. Four of them are black. You put the marbles back. There are a total of 200 marbles in the bag. Based on your handful, how many of the marbles in the bag will be black?

Write an Equation

You can write an equation to answer test questions about proportions.

Example

Daniella designs pages for a fashion magazine. She puts seven photos on every five pages. How many photos will she put in a 50-page magazine?

STEP 1 Write a proportion to model the problem. Let n represent the number of photos in a 50-page magazine.

$$\text{number of photos} \rightarrow \frac{7}{5} = \frac{n}{50} \leftarrow \text{number of photos}$$
$$\text{number of pages} \rightarrow \qquad\qquad \leftarrow \text{number of pages}$$

STEP 2 Use cross products to write an equation.

$$\frac{7}{5} = \frac{n}{50}$$
$$7 \times 50 = 5 \times n$$
$$350 = 5n$$

STEP 3 Solve for n.

Daniella will put 70 photos in a 50-page magazine.

$$350 = 5n$$
$$350 \div 5 = 5n \div 5$$
$$70 = n$$

TRY IT OUT

At a grocery store 2 out of every 3 customers use the self-checkout. If 120 customers are at the store, how many will use the self-checkout?

Circle the correct answer.

A. 360   B. 240   C. 120   D. 80

Option D is correct. Eighty customers will use the self-checkout because when you solve the proportion $\frac{2}{3} = \frac{n}{120}$, $n = 80$.

Use the drawing to write each ratio.

1. number of baseballs to footballs

2. number of footballs to all balls

Write the ratio.

3. the number of even digits to odd digits in this group of numbers: 2, 3, 5, 7, 8

4. the number of vowels to the number of consonants in the name CONSTANCE

Solve.

5. In 8 servings of granola cereal, there are 56 grams of fat. How many grams of fat per serving is that?

6. Dmitri can read 45 pages in 30 minutes. What is his reading rate in pages per minute? In pages per hour?

Tell whether the statement is a proportion.

7. $\frac{3}{8} = \frac{9}{32}$

8. $\frac{12}{15} = \frac{4}{5}$

Solve.

9. Loni gets paid $51 for 3 hours of work. Adam gets paid $36 for 2 hours of work. Do Loni and Adam get paid at the same rate? If not, whose rate is higher?

10. Jerome did 36 push-ups in 1 minute. Will did 54 push-ups in 1.5 minutes. Did they do push-ups at the same rate? If not, whose rate was higher?

Solve for *n*.

11. $\frac{5}{24} = \frac{15}{n}$

12. $\frac{n}{18} = \frac{10}{12}$

13. $\frac{8}{n} = \frac{6}{3}$

Write a proportion and solve each problem.

14. You can bowl 5 games for $7.50. How many games can you bowl for $30?

15. There are 24 tennis balls in 8 packages. How many are in 5 packages?

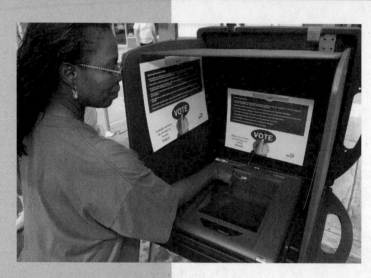

Real-Life Matters

In the United States, citizens can register to vote when they turn 18. Once registered, a citizen can then vote in local and national elections.

Voting is very important. However, not all people who can vote actually do. In a recent election for president, only 51% of U.S. citizens voted. Would you consider that a large or a small percentage?

Percent means *per hundred*. You can think of a percent as a fraction with a denominator of 100. So, 51% means $\frac{51}{100}$, or 51 out of 100.

Real-Life Application

Your friend is running for class president. You set a goal to get at least 75% of the students to vote. The school has 940 students. Is 75% a large or small part of the total number of students? Explain.

_____

How do you find out how many votes 75% is of the total 940?

_____

Your younger brother does *not* know what a percent is. He does know what fractions and decimals are. How do you explain to him what 75% is as a fraction? How do you explain how to write 75% as a decimal?

_____

_____

_____

Overview • Lessons 8–10

Fractions and Percents

Fractions name parts of a whole. Suppose 5 people, or candidates, run for mayor. Two candidates are men and 3 are women. You can say that $\frac{2}{5}$ of the candidates are men and $\frac{3}{5}$ of the candidates are women.

In this example, there are only 5 people in all. However, as groups get larger, fractions may not be the best way to show the parts. *Percents* work better.

Imagine that 20,400 people voted in the election for mayor, 11,730 of them voted for your favorite person. You could say that $\frac{11,730}{20,400}$ of the people voted for your favorite candidate. This fraction is not easy to understand. A percent, on the other hand, tells you how many people <u>out of 100</u> voted for your favorite candidate. Your candidate received 57.5% of the vote.

In the next lesson you will learn more about percents. You will learn how to write fractions as percents and percents as fractions. You will also learn how to write the same information using percents and fractions.

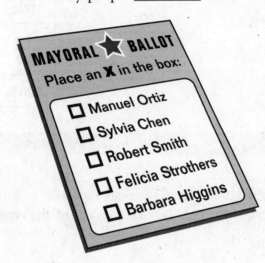

MAYORAL ★ BALLOT
Place an **X** in the box:
☐ Manuel Ortiz
☐ Sylvia Chen
☐ Robert Smith
☐ Felicia Strothers
☐ Barbara Higgins

YOU KNOW

- A fraction names a part of a whole
- That equivalent fractions name the same number
- That fractions and decimals can name the same number
- How to simplify a fraction
- That two equivalent ratios form a proportion

YOU WILL LEARN

- That percents and fractions show a ratio out of 100
- How to use proportions to write fractions as percents
- How to write percents as fractions

Remember the BASICS

Write each ratio as a fraction in simplest form.

1. 4 out of 12

$$\frac{4}{12} = \frac{4}{12} \div \frac{4}{4} = \frac{1}{3}$$

2. 60 out of 100

3. 8 out of 20

4. 0.75

5. 0.55

6. 0.07

LESSON 8 Understanding Percents

At a discount store, Mia purchased this dog collar on sale.

What percent of a dollar did she spend?

You know that a dollar is 100 cents. When you compare a number to 100 it is called a **percent**. Percent (%) means *per hundred*. You can write the ratio $\frac{39}{100}$ as 39%.

Mia spent 39 cents or $\frac{39}{100}$ or 39% of her dollar.

Some percents are easy to understand and remember.

> 100% of something means *all of it*.
> 0% of something is *none* of it.

dollar	dime	quarter
$1.00	$0.10	$0.25
100¢	10¢	25¢
$\frac{100}{100}$	$\frac{10}{100}$	$\frac{25}{100}$
100%	10%	25%

Example

You paid $100 to have your car repaired. $15 of the bill was for a car part. The cost of the part is what percent of the repair bill?

STEP 1 Write a ratio.

$$\frac{\$15}{\$100}$$

STEP 2 Write this ratio as a percent.

$$\frac{15}{100} = 15\%$$

$15 is 15% of the bill.

ON YOUR OWN

One hundred students tried out for the school play. Twenty-two of the students got a part in the play. Write this ratio as a percent.

Practice

Building Skills

Write each as a percent.

1. 44¢ as part of a dollar

    $$\frac{44¢}{100¢} = \frac{44}{100}$$
    $$\frac{44}{100} = 44\%$$

2. 58 out of 100 rock musicians

3. 91 out of 100 soccer players

4. $30 out of $100

5. 75¢ as part of a dollar

6. 85 wins in 100 games

7. 66 out of 100 singers

8. 92 out of 100 questions answered correctly

9. 53 girls in a class of 100 students

10. 14 lost out of 100 sent

Problem Solving

Find the percent.

11. Carlos has a dollar. He spends 50¢ on a pen. What percent of a dollar did he spend?

    $$\frac{50¢}{100¢} = \frac{50}{100} = 50\%$$

12. A salesperson earns a $17 bonus each time she sells a $100 item. What percentage bonus does the salesperson earn?

13. In the United States, some people pay $0.23 out of every $1.00 they make to pay taxes. What percentage of $1.00 do these people pay in tax?

14. A local softball team won 46 of the 100 games it played. What percentage of games did the team *win*?

Converting Fractions to Percents

In the last lesson, you learned how to change a fraction to a percent when the denominator is 100. In fact, *you can write any fraction as a percent.*

To change a fraction to a percent you can

- Multiply by 100%

$$\frac{3}{4} \times 100\% = \frac{3}{4} \times \frac{100}{1} = \frac{75}{1} = 75\%$$

- Divide, move the decimal 2 places, and write a % sign

$$\frac{3}{4} = 4)\overline{3.00} = 75\%$$
$$-28$$
$$\quad 20$$
$$\quad 20$$

Example

Ahmad got 6 answers correct out of 8 questions on a math quiz. What percent did Ahmad get correct?

STEP 1 Set up the fraction.
$$\frac{6}{8}$$

STEP 2 Multiply OR divide.

$$\frac{6}{8} = 8)\overline{6.00} = 75\% \quad \text{OR} \quad \frac{6}{8} \times 100\% = \frac{6}{8} \times \frac{100}{1} = \frac{75}{1} = 75\%$$
$$-56$$
$$\quad 40$$
$$\quad 40$$

Ahmed scored 75%.

ON YOUR OWN

Germaine played a video game. In the game, she hit 12 of the 20 targets. What percentage of the targets did she hit?

Practice

Simplify fractions before you begin to solve.

Building Skills

Write each fraction as a percent.

1. $\dfrac{4}{5}$

    $$\dfrac{4}{5} \times 100$$

    $$\dfrac{4}{\underset{1}{\cancel{5}}} \times \overset{20}{\cancel{100}} = 80\%$$

2. $\dfrac{9}{10}$

3. $\dfrac{11}{20}$

4. $\dfrac{3}{50}$

5. $\dfrac{3}{8}$

6. $\dfrac{22}{100}$

7. $\dfrac{64}{200}$

8. $\dfrac{14}{20}$

9. $\dfrac{80}{400}$

Problem Solving

Solve.

10. There are 20 members in the school chorus. Seventeen had never been in the chorus before. What percentage of the members had never been in the chorus before?

    $$\dfrac{17}{20} = \dfrac{17}{\underset{1}{\cancel{20}}} \times \dfrac{\overset{5}{\cancel{100}}}{1} = 85\%$$

11. To pass the written part of the driver's test in Nevada, you need to answer 40 out of 50 questions correctly. What percentage of questions must be answered correctly?

12. There are 40 students helping with after-school tutoring. Twenty-eight of the students are juniors and seniors. What percentage are juniors and seniors?

13. A survey shows that $\dfrac{7}{8}$ of mall shoppers use discount coupons. What percentage of mall shoppers use discount coupons?

14. Twenty-four hikers out of 400 hikers got poison ivy. What percentage of the hikers got poison ivy?

15. A skateboarder cleanly performs a new move 16 out of 80 tries. What percentage of the time does she cleanly perform the move?

LESSON 10 Converting Percents to Fractions

Writing a percent as a fraction is easier than writing a fraction as a percent.

You only need to remember how to simplify a fraction.

To write any percent as a fraction:

- Write the percent as a fraction with a *denominator* of 100.
- Simplify the fraction if possible.

> Remember percent means *per hundred*. So any percent can be written in the fraction form $\frac{n}{100}$.

Example

Thirty percent of the students attend a driver's ed class after school. What fraction of students attend driver's ed after school?

STEP 1 Write the percent as a fraction with a denominator of 100.

$$30\% = \frac{30}{100}$$

STEP 2 Simplify the fraction if possible. Divide the numerator and denominator by their greatest common factor (GCF).
Factors of 30 are 1, 2, 3, 5, 6, **10**, 15, 30
Factors of 100 are 1, 2, 4, 5, **10**, 20, 25, 50, 100
The GCF of 30 and 100 is 10.

$$\frac{30}{100} \rightarrow \frac{30 \div \mathbf{10}}{100 \div \mathbf{10}} \rightarrow \frac{3}{10}$$

$\frac{3}{10}$ of the students attend driver's ed after school.

ON YOUR OWN

In this year's graduating class, 85% of the students plan on going to college. What fraction of the students plans to go to college?

Practice

Building Skills

Write each percent as a fraction.

1. 55%

$$55\% = \frac{55}{100}$$

$$\frac{55 \div 5}{100 \div 5} = \frac{11}{20}$$

2. 95%

3. 15%

4. 44%

5. 83%

6. 28%

7. 8%

8. 34%

9. 68%

Problem Solving

Solve.

10. Forty-five percent of the teachers at your school can name at least one popular recording artist. What fraction of the teachers is this?

$$45\% = \frac{45}{100} = \frac{9}{20}$$

11. On a game show, one contestant correctly answered 43% of the questions. What fraction of the questions did she answer correctly?

12. Only 15% of the school clean-up committee members are new. What fraction of the members is new?

13. In a survey, 68% of students said that they collect trading cards. What fraction of the students collects trading cards?

14. At the 2002 Winter Olympics, 29% of the medals won by the United States were gold medals. What fraction of the medals won were gold medals?

15. Maureen is saving 28% of her pay for a class trip to the beach. What fraction of her pay is she saving for the trip?

TEST–TAKING STRATEGY

Use a Graph

You can use a graph to answer test questions about percents.

The circle graph shows the materials dropped off at a recycling center last month.

What fraction of the materials is plastic bottles?

STEP 1 Locate plastic bottles on the circle graph. Write the percent.
35%

STEP 2 Write the percent as a fraction with a denominator of 100.

$35\% = \dfrac{35}{100}$

STEP 3 Write the fraction in simplest form. Remember, to write a fraction in simplest form you need to find the greatest common factor (GCF) of the two numbers forming the fraction. In this case, the GCF is 5.

$\dfrac{35}{100} \div \dfrac{5}{5} = \dfrac{7}{20}$

$\dfrac{7}{20}$ of the materials are plastic bottles.

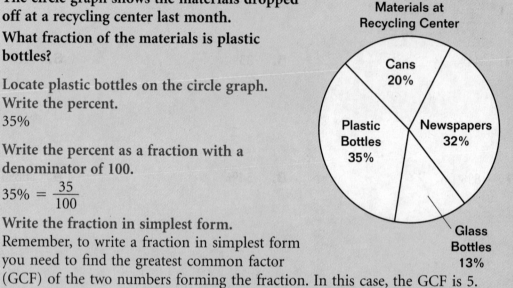

Materials at Recycling Center

Cans 20%

Plastic Bottles 35%

Newspapers 32%

Glass Bottles 13%

TRY IT OUT

Use the circle graph above. What part of the materials at the recycling center are cans?

Circle the correct answer.

A. $\dfrac{2}{100}$ B. $\dfrac{1}{50}$ C. $\dfrac{1}{5}$ D. $\dfrac{20}{10}$

Option C is correct. 20% of the materials are cans, $20\% = \dfrac{20}{100} = \dfrac{1}{5}$

Overview • Lessons 11–12

Decimals and Percents

You can write percents as fractions and fractions as percents. In some problems fractions work best. At other times, percents work best.

The lunch bill for you and your friends comes to $25. You want to leave an 18% tip. You need to find 18% of $25.

One way to solve this problem is to write 18% as a decimal. Then you need to multiply it by $25.

Sometimes, it is more useful to use a percent. You read that your favorite basketball player has a 0.180 3-point shot average. Is this good? If you read that this player successfully shoots 3-pointers 18% of the time, would this be easier to understand? His rate is less than 20%, or about 1 out of 5. It is easier to see now that this rate is not a very good one.

Next you will learn to change decimals to percents and change percents to decimals.

YOU KNOW

- That percent means "per hundred"

- That fractions and decimals can name the same number

YOU WILL LEARN

- How to write any decimal as a percent

- How to write any percent as a decimal

Remember the BASICS

Write each fraction as a percent. Write each percent as a fraction in simplest form.

1. $\dfrac{3}{12} = \dfrac{n}{100}$

$$\dfrac{12n}{12} = \dfrac{300}{12}$$
$$n = 25$$
$$\dfrac{3}{12} = 25\%$$

2. $\dfrac{6}{15}$

3. $\dfrac{8}{40}$

4. 72%

5. 45%

6. 36%

Converting Decimals to Percents

A survey of high school students found that 0.74 favor having a student lounge. What percent of those surveyed favor having a student lounge?

You can write *any* decimal as a percent. Here are the steps to write 0.74 as a percent.

• Multiply the decimal by 100. This moves the decimal point 2 places to the right.

> $0.74 \times 100 = 074 = 74$

• Write a percent sign.

> $0.74 = 74\%$

74% of the students favor having a student lounge.

Example

A customer calculated that 0.294 people in a grocery store buy green beans. What percent of people in the store buy green beans?

STEP 1 Multiply the decimal by 100. This moves the decimal point *2 places to the right*.

> $0.294 \times 100 = 0.29.4 \longrightarrow 29.4$ Drop zeros that are not needed.

STEP 2 Write the percent sign.

> $0.294 = 29.4\%$

ON YOUR OWN

According to a survey, 0.8 of the students in Neela's school like the idea of extending the school day to 5:00 PM. What percent of students want to extend the school day?

Practice

Move the decimal point 2 places to the right to convert a decimal to a percent.

Building Skills

Write each decimal as a percent.

1. 0.06

$$0.06 = 0.06 = 6\%$$

2. 0.64

3. 0.052

4. 0.888

5. 0.7

6. 0.005

7. 0.0024

8. 0.908

9. 1.4

10. 1.063

Problem Solving

Solve.

11. In Serena's class, 0.45 of the students do not want to go to school through July. What is 0.45 written as a percent?

$$0.45 = 45\%$$

12. Your friend estimates that about 0.95 of the kids in his high school would like to order take-out food for lunch. What percent of the students is that?

13. Out of all the members of the school drama club, only 0.35 can sing, dance, and act. What percent of the drama club can sing, dance, and act?

14. In a survey of high school seniors, 0.05 said that they would like to spend another year at school. What percent of the seniors surveyed would like to stay in high school for another year?

15. In a survey that Golda took, 0.652 of the people she surveyed said that students should take a class about money. What percent of the people that Golda surveyed *did not* think that the class would be useful?

16. Of the 400 students in Moira's class, 0.98 of them say that they plan to become teachers. What percent is this?

LESSON 12 — Converting Percents to Decimals

Sometimes to solve a problem it is easier to work with percents that have been changed to decimals. You can write any percent as a decimal.

- Get rid of the percent sign. Add a decimal point if needed. A decimal point to the right of a whole number does not change its value.

- Move the decimal point *2* places to the *left*. Sometimes you may need to add a zero as a placeholder.

Why did you move the decimal? When you wrote decimals as percents, you moved the decimal point 2 places to the right. Now, when you change percents to decimals, you will move the decimal point in the opposite direction: 2 places to the left. Remember, *percent* means *per hundred* or *divided by one hundred*.

Example

Only 6% of teens questioned said that watching movies at home is better than seeing them in the theater. What is 6% percent written as a decimal?

STEP 1 Remove the percent sign.
6% = 6.

STEP 2 Move the decimal point two places to the left.

6. ⟶ 0.06.

It is also correct to write a 0 to the left of the decimal point in the ones place.

6% written as a decimal is 0.06.

ON YOUR OWN

The newspaper reported that 25.5% of people surveyed watched the news every night. How would you write this as a decimal?

Practice

Move the decimal point 2 places to the left to convert a percent to a decimal.

Building Skills

Write each percent as a decimal.

1. 85%

$85\% = 85.$
$85. \rightarrow 0.85$
$85\% = 0.85$

2. 65%

3. 12%

4. 48%

5. 73%

6. 29%

7. 4%

8. 34.7%

9. 150%

10. 2.5%

11. 3.1%

12. 0.3%

Problem Solving

Solve.

13. According to a survey, 74% of teens believe that the prices for a movie are too high. How would you write that percent as a decimal?

$74\% = .74 = 0.74$

14. Moviegoers agree that prices are 40% too high. What decimal is equal to this percent?

15. Teens were asked about their favorite kinds of movies. Forty-eight percent said that comedies were their favorite. What is the decimal equivalent?

16. Of teens surveyed, only 5% said that movie theaters charge fair prices for popcorn and candy. Write this percent as a decimal.

17. A movie critic has given a thumbs-up to 62.5% of the movies she has rated. Write a decimal equal to the percent of movies that she did *not* like.

18. A young filmmaker says that she always gives a 120% effort on every film she shoots. What decimal is equal to 120%?

TEST-TAKING STRATEGY

Draw a Number Line

Drawing a number line can help you answer test questions about percents and decimals.

Example

Students were asked how frequently they use credit cards. The table shows their responses.

Credit Card Use			
Never	Seldom	Often	Always
0.031	0.64	0.069	0.26

Which response did more than 60% of the students give?

STEP 1 Change each decimal to a percent.

0.031	0.64	0.069	0.26
↓	↓	↓	↓
3.1%	64%	6.9%	26%

STEP 2 Draw a number line.
For this problem you would draw a number line from 0% to 100%.

STEP 3 Mark the approximate location of each percent on a number line.

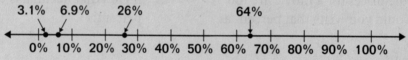

STEP 4 Use the number line to find the percent greater than 60%.
64%

More than 60% of the students gave the response *Seldom*.

TRY IT OUT

The air we breathe is made up of 0.21 oxygen, 0.78 nitrogen, and 0.01 other gases. Which gas makes up more than 50% of the air?

Circle the correct answer.

A. oxygen   B. nitrogen   C. other gases   D. not here

Option B is correct. 0.78 of the air is nitrogen.
0.78 = 78% which is greater than 50%

Overview • Lessons 13–15

Percents and Problem Solving I

Now that you have learned how to convert fractions, decimals, and percents, you can begin to understand and solve percent problems.

You already know that fractions and decimals are used to show parts of a whole. A percent also shows part of a whole.

$$\frac{\text{Part}}{\text{Whole}} \times 100 = \text{Percent}$$

Look at the pizza. If you take 2 of the slices, you take

$$\frac{2}{8} = \frac{1}{4} = 0.25 = 25\%$$

To solve percent problems on tests, there are three pieces of information that you need: the whole, the part, and the percent.

Look at the pizza again. We can say that the
- whole = 8 slices
- part = 2 slices
- percent = 25%

YOU KNOW
- That percent means *out of 100*
- How to convert percents, fractions, and decimals

YOU WILL LEARN
- How to find the whole, the part, and the percent
- A strategy to help solve percent problems

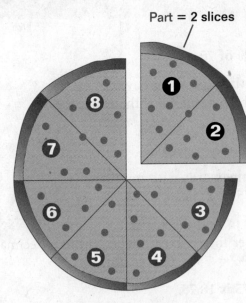

Part = 2 slices

Whole = 8 slices

Remember the BASICS

Fill in the chart below with equivalent fractions, decimals, and percents.

FRACTION	DECIMAL	PERCENT
$\frac{1}{1}$	1.00	100%
	0.75	
		66%
	0.17	
		20%
$\frac{7}{8}$		

When you are solving percent problems, you're looking for a missing piece. The percent triangle helps you to find that piece. A percent triangle shows how the three pieces are related.

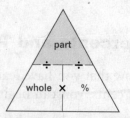

Look at the triangle. To find the part, cover the word part. The remaining pieces are connected by a multiplication sign. Multiply the pieces you have to find the part.

Example

Find 25% of 75.

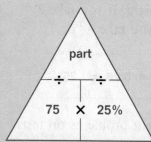

STEP 1 Identify the pieces you have.
25% is the percent. 75 is the whole.

STEP 2 Write a percent sentence.
part = whole × percent.

STEP 3 Replace the words with numbers.
part = 75 × 25%

STEP 4 Multiply to find the answer.
Remember to convert your percent to a decimal.
75 × 25% = 75 × 0.25 = 18.75.

25% of 75 is 18.75.

ON YOUR OWN

There are 60 students in Mr. Watt's math class. 65% of them have jobs after school. How many students have jobs after school?

Practice

Building Skills

Find the part.

1. 82% of 50

   50 × 82%
   50 × 0.82 = 41

2. 31% of 66

3. 10% of 45

4. 50% of 600

5. 23% of 90

6. 2.5% of 22

7. 60% of 60

8. 64.7% of 12

9. 150% of 4

Problem Solving

Solve.

10. Twenty-eight percent of the 150 students in the senior class are either on a team or in a club. How many seniors are either on a team or in a club?

    part = 150 × 0.28 = 42

11. Seventy-five percent of the actors in a play are on stage for the first time. There are 32 actors in the play. How many are on stage for the first time?

12. There are 40 stores in the mall. Of these stores, 62.5% sell clothing. How many stores in the mall sell clothing?

13. In one baseball game, 37.5% of the balls hit were fly balls. If 24 balls were hit in that game, how many were fly balls?

14. You are collecting for a local charity. Seventy percent of the 140 houses that you called on made a promise, or pledge, to give money. How many houses made a pledge?

15. A company's sales goal for March is $250,000. The company reached 80% of that goal. What was the amount of their sales in March?

LESSON 14   Find the Whole

Sixteen teens have after-school jobs at a local video store. This is 20% of the students who applied for jobs. How many teens applied for jobs at the video store?

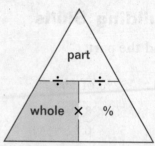

You used the percent triangle to help you find the part. Sometimes you will be asked to find the whole. The percent triangle can help you find the whole, too.

To find the whole, cover the word *whole*. The remaining pieces are connected with a division sign. Divide the part by the percent to find the whole. Remember to rewrite the percent as a decimal before you divide.

Example

30 is 60% of what number?

STEP 1   Identify the pieces you have.
30 is the part. 60% is the percent.

STEP 2   Write a percent sentence.
whole = part ÷ percent.

STEP 3   Replace the words with numbers.
whole = 30 ÷ 60%

STEP 4   Divide to find the answer.
30 ÷ 60% = 30 ÷ 0.60 = 50

30 is 60% of 50.

ON YOUR OWN

12 is 24% of what number?

Practice

Building Skills

Find the whole.

1. Forty-two is 50% of what number?

whole = 42 ÷ 50% = 42 ÷ 0.50 = 84

2. Forty-eight is 40% of what number?

3. Ninety is 30% of what number?

4. Fifteen is 125% of what number?

Find _n_. (Think of _n_ as _what number_?)

5. Twenty-five percent of _n_ is 20.

6. One hundred-twenty percent of _n_ is 18.

7. One hundred-twenty is 125% of _n_.

8. Twenty-five percent of _n_ is 72.

Problem Solving

Solve.

9. Twenty-four college students were hired as ushers for a concert. This is 30% of the students who applied for the job. How many college students applied to be ushers?

whole = 24 ÷ 30%
whole = 24 ÷ 0.30
whole = 80

10. Thirty-two businesses in town receive an award for supporting the community. This is 16% of all of the businesses in town. How many businesses are there in town?

11. Six percent of those who applied were accepted into the summer-study program at the college. Three hundred were accepted. How many applied?

12. Three hundred-thirty deer were counted by park rangers. This is 165% of the number expected. How many deer did park rangers expect to count?

13. Forty-five parents, which is 37.5% of all the parents, came to see the school play. How many parents are there in all?

14. Seventy-five of the students who entered the art contest won prizes. This is $12\frac{1}{2}$% of all the students who entered. How many students entered the contest?

Find the Percent

Two hundred radio listeners called in to name their favorite group. Forty named the same group as their favorite. What percent of those who called in named this group?

You have used the percent triangle to find the part and to find the whole. Now you can use the percent triangle to find the percent.

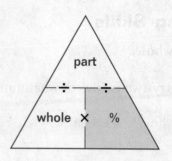

To find the percent, cover the symbol for *percent*. The remaining pieces are connected with a division sign. Divide the part by the whole to find the percent. The answer is a decimal. Multiply the decimal by 100 to find the percent form.

Example

Thirty-three is what percent of 150?

STEP 1 Identify the pieces you have.
Thirty-three is the part. One hundred-fifty is the whole.

STEP 2 Write a percent sentence.
percent = (part ÷ whole) × 100

STEP 3 Replace the words with numbers.
percent = (33 ÷ 150) × 100

STEP 4 Divide. Then multiply by 100 and add the % sign.
(33 ÷ 150) × 100 = 0.22 × 100 = 22%

33 is 22% of 150.

ON YOUR OWN

What percent of 88 is 22?

Practice

Building Skills

Find each percent.

1. What percent of 240 is 60?

   percent = (60 ÷ 240) × 100
   0.25 × 100 = 25%

2. What percent of 240 is 90?

3. What percent of 288 is 72?

4. What percent of 200 is 140?

5. What percent of 360 is 18?

6. Thirteen is what percent of 80?

7. Twenty-seven is what percent of 50?

8. Six is what percent of 40?

9. Forty is what percent of 25?

10. Twelve is what percent of 75?

Problem Solving

Solve.

11. Only 400 of 1,200 teens chose country music as their favorite type of music. What percent of the teens chose country music?

    percent = (part ÷ whole) × 100
    percent = (400 ÷ 1,200) × 100
    percent = (0.33) × 100
    percent = 33%

12. A disc jockey plays 48 different songs at a party. Thirty-six of those songs are fast songs. What percent of the songs played are fast songs?

13. Thirty-two students are invited to go sightseeing. However, 144 students show up! Describe the number who came to go sightseeing as a percent of those who were invited. *Hint:* The answer is more than 100%.

14. Fifty-six of 224 passengers on an airplane slept on the flight. What percent of the passengers got some sleep?

TEST–TAKING STRATEGY

Draw a Diagram

Drawing the percent triangle will help you answer test questions about percents.

Example

To pass her history test, Jolene must answer 80% of the questions correctly. There are 80 questions on the test. How many questions must she answer correctly to pass the test?

STEP 1 Draw the percent triangle.

STEP 2 Identify the pieces you have.
You are given the whole, 80 questions, and you are given the percent, 80%. You are looking for the part. Cover *part* in the triangle.

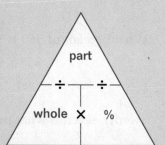

STEP 3 Write a percent sentence.
part = whole × percent.

STEP 4 Replace the words with numbers.
part = 80 × 80%.

STEP 5 Multiply.
80 × 80% = 80 × 0.80 = 64.

Jolene will have to answer 64 questions correctly to pass.

TRY IT OUT

A bill for cable TV is $60. Of that amount, 80% is for basic cable service. The rest is for movie channels. About how much does basic cable service cost?

Circle the correct answer.

A. $55   B. $4.80   C. $7.50   D. $48

Option D is correct. $60 (whole) × 80% (percent) = 60 × 0.8 = $48 (part).

Overview • Lessons **16–17**

Percents and Problem Solving II

You just got a test back. However your teacher did not give you a grade or a percentage. All you know is you answered 55 questions correctly and answered 5 incorrectly. How would you find out the percent of the questions answered correctly?

You have learned how to solve 3 types of percent problems. You solve each by using a different method.

- Find the part
  part = whole × percent

- Find the whole
  whole = part ÷ percent

- Find the percent
  percent = (part ÷ whole) × 100

Now you will learn how to solve *any type* of percent problem by using a percent equation.

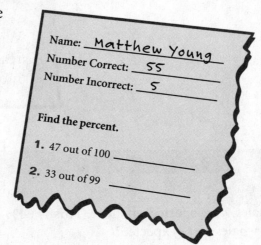

Name: Matthew Young
Number Correct: 55
Number Incorrect: 5

Find the percent.

1. 47 out of 100 _____

2. 33 out of 99 _____

YOU KNOW

- How to multiply to find the percent of a number

- How to set up and solve a proportion

- How to find a number when you know a percent and part of the number

- How to find the percent that one number is to another number

- How to write an equation and then solve it for *n* (missing number)

YOU WILL LEARN

- What a percent equation is

- How to write a percent equation from a word problem

Remember the BASICS

Solve each equation for *n*.

1. $25n = 400$

$$\frac{25n}{25} = \frac{400}{25}$$

$$n = 16$$

2. $n = 0.2 - 120$

3. $49 = 0.6n$

4. $\frac{n}{1.2} = 30$

5. $3.6 = 0.9n$

6. $2.4 + 4 = 0.8n$

LESSON 16 What Is a Percent Equation?

You have worked with different equations to find the missing piece in a percent problem. There is another way to solve percent problems. Use a **percent equation** to solve any type of percent problem. Write the equation as simply as you can. Use the **variable,** n, to stand for the missing number.

The rules on the right will help you.

Rules for Reading and Writing a Percent Equation

1. Restate the question as simply as possible. Replace any percent in the problem with a decimal.

2. Write the equation the way you read the problem. Use n for the missing number.

Example

30 whales were spotted offshore. This is 60% of the total expected. How many whales were expected?

STEP 1 Restate the problem as simply as possible. Replace any percent with a decimal.
30 is 0.6 of what number?

STEP 2 Write the equation the way you read the problem. Use n for the missing number.
$30 = 0.6 \times n$

30	is	0.6	of	what number?
30	=	0.6	×	n

STEP 3 Solve for n.
$$30 = 0.6 \times n$$
$$\frac{30}{0.6} = \frac{0.6}{0.6} \times n$$
$$50 = n$$

50 whales were expected.

ON YOUR OWN

Last year Ms. Salas had 30 students in her class. There were 120 students in the school. What percent of the students were in Ms. Salas' class?

Practice

Building Skills

Write a percent equation to solve each problem.

1. What percent of 60 is 24?

   $$n \times 60 = 24$$
   $$60n = 24$$

2. What is 32% of 80?

3. What percent of 64 is 12?

4. Eighty percent of what number is 16?

5. What percent of 240 is 180?

6. What is 28% of 54?

7. Sixty-two percent of what number is 16?

8. Sixty is what percent of 20?

9. What is 2% of 10?

10. Ten percent of what number is 12?

11. What percent of 3.6 is 1.8?

12. What is 2.2% of 200?

13. Forty-four percent of what number is 22?

14. Sixteen is what percent of 68?

15. What is 2.32% of 50?

16. Seventy-five percent of what number is 33?

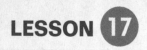
Creating a Percent Equation from a Word Problem

A word problem can be solved using a percent equation, too. First, cut out all the details when you rewrite the problem. Then, use the numbers that you have. Usually you are given two numbers and asked to find the third number. You can replace the word *percent* with the word *decimal*. This reminds you that your answer, *n*, will be the decimal form of the percent.

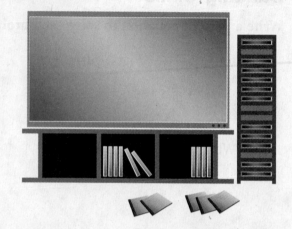

Example

Maureen has a collection of 80 DVDs. She loaned 16 of them to her friends. What percent of the DVDs did she loan?

STEP 1 Say the question as simply as possible. Replace any percent with a decimal.
What percent of 80 is 16?
What decimal of 80 is 16?

STEP 2 Write the equation the way you read the problem. Use *n* for the missing number and solve.
$n \times 80 = 16$
$n = 0.2 = .2 \times 100 = 20\%$

Maureen loaned 20% of her DVD collection.

ON YOUR OWN

In a parade, 1,170 marchers each carry a musical instrument. This is 65% of the total marchers. How many marchers are in the parade?

Practice

Building Skills

Write a percent equation to solve each problem.

1. The mail carrier delivers the mail to 44 of the houses on Warren Street. This is 20% of all the houses on Warren Street. How many houses are on Warren Street?

> 44 is 0.2 of what number?
> $44 = 0.2 \times n$
> $44 = 0.2n$
> $220 = n$

2. Latisha saves 30% of her monthly take-home pay to buy a set of drums. Her monthly take-home pay is $1,340. How much does she save each month?

3. A professional volleyball team won 28 games and lost 22. What percent of their games did they lose?

4. Enrico sold 55 postcards from his collection. This was 11% of his collection. How many postcards did he have before he sold any?

5. A city recycles 85% of the newspapers sold there. The total amount of newspapers sold comes to 8 tons. How many tons get recycled?

6. Leanna spent $50 to buy hats with her school's name on them. She sold them all for a total of $175. By what percent did her money increase?

7. Eighteen students in the school system are new to the United States. This is 0.2% of all the students. How many students are in the school system?

8. In a beach volleyball play-off, 28% of the players are in a play-off for the first time. There are 145 players. How many are in their first play-off?

9. In one college, 386 of the 623 graduating seniors had jobs lined up after graduation. What percent of the seniors had jobs lined up?

10. In one study 94.5% of the people who do *not* exercise regularly said that they do not feel their best. Poor muscle tone was found in 821 of the people studied. How many total people were in the study?

TEST–TAKING STRATEGY

Check for Reasonableness of an Answer

You can check for the reasonableness of an answer when you answer test questions about percents.

Example

There are 824 students in a high school graduating class. Out of that class, 580 students plan to attend college. About what percent of the graduating class plans to attend college?

STEP 1 Read and restate the question.
You know the part of the graduating class planning to attend college (580) and the whole, or total number of students in the graduating class (824). You need to write the number of graduating students who plan to attend college as a percent.

STEP 2 Make a plan to solve the problem.
You need to estimate a percentage based on the numbers that you know. Round 824 to 800 and 580 to 600 to make the numbers easier to use.

STEP 3 Do the plan. Divide to find the percent.
You find the percentage by dividing 600 students planning to attend college by the total 800 students.

$$\frac{600}{800} = \frac{3}{4} = 75\%$$

STEP 4 Check the answer.
Is the answer reasonable? The answer for $\frac{580}{824}$ is about 70.4%, so 75% is a reasonable answer.

About 75% of the students plan to attend college.

TRY IT OUT

The enrollment at a technical school is 789. Out of these students, 391 own a car. About what percent of the students own a car?

Circle the correct answer.

A. about 10%   **B.** about 40%   **C.** about 50%   **D.** about 100%

Option C is correct. $\frac{391}{789} = 49.6\%$, $\frac{400}{800} = \frac{4}{8} = \frac{1}{2}$ or 50%
The answer 50% is reasonable.

Find the percent.

1. 47 out of 100

2. 88 of 100 questions answered correctly on a test

Write each fraction as a percent and each percent as a fraction in simplest form.

3. $\dfrac{13}{20}$

4. $\dfrac{280}{400}$

5. 36%

Write each decimal as a percent and each percent as a decimal.

6. 0.42

7. 61%

8. 4.8%

Solve.

9. Find 42% of 400.

10. Forty is what percent of 25?

11. Eighteen is 40% of what number?

12. Twenty is what percent of 20?

13. Erin sold 40% of her collection of 80 CDs. How many CDs did she sell?

14. Inez spent $162 at the clothing store. This is 75% of what Tanya spent at the same store. How much did Tanya spend?

Write an equation you could use to solve each problem.

15. What percent of 18 is 8?

16. Nina worked for 6 hours at the shop this week. That number of hours is 20% of the number she plans to work during the holiday season. How many hours per week does Nina plan to work during the holidays?

UNIT 3

Percents in Daily Life

Real-Life Matters

In the grocery store, a package says *30% more free.* How do you know if you really got 30% more? A sign at the mall says *Take another 10% off our already low prices.* How do you know if that 10% discount makes a big difference in the price?

Real-Life Application

Suppose you are shopping for some new clothes for your part-time job. You find a pair of slacks that are marked $20. The sign above the rack says *ticketed price is 20% off.* The original price on the tag was $30. Is the store's sign correct? How do you know?

_____

_____

Percents are part of everyday life.

Later on, you find the perfect shoes for only $33. You don't have enough money but the store offers a deal. You can pay half now and half next week, but they charge a $5 fee. Another store has the same shoes for 10% off the original price of $42, and they charge no fee. Which store has the better deal?

_____

_____

Knowing how to apply percents will help you in all aspects of your life.

At the foodcourt, one place offers 5 chicken wings, a small salad, and drink for $4.95. The place next door has a sign that says *We'll give you 20% more chicken wings for the same price.* You order your meal from them and are surprised to see 7 chicken wings. Is the store's sign correct? Explain.

_____

_____

Overview • Lessons 18–19

Application of Percents I

The more you know about solving percent problems, the better you will be at solving everyday questions. The manager of a clothing store lowers the price of denim jackets from $125 to $100. She wants to advertise the sale. What percent reduction is this?

You can write a percent equation.

> 25 is what percent of 125? or
>
> $25 = n \times 125$

Solve for n. The answer is a decimal.

> $25 = n \times 125 = \dfrac{25}{125} = n = 0.2$

You change the decimal to a percent by moving the decimal point 2 places to the right and adding the percent sign.

> $0.2 = 20\%$

The sale price for denim jackets is 20% off.

BIG SALE!

Denim Jackets
WERE $125.00

NOW
$100.00

YOU KNOW

- How to find the percent of a number
- How to find the whole if you have the percent and the part
- How to use a percent equation to solve a problem

YOU WILL LEARN

- How to find the percent of increase or decrease
- How to find the markup or discount

Remember the BASICS

Solve. The first one is done for you.

1. What is 20% of $120?	$n = 0.2 \times 120 = 24$ $n = \$24$ 20% of $120 = $24.	**2.** What percent of $96 is $16?
3. What percent of $40 is $32?		**4.** $15 is 30% of what dollar amount?
5. $12 is 40% of what dollar amount?		**6.** What is 25% of $550?

LESSON 18 Percent Change

When you find a percent change, you are comparing a number and the amount that the number changes. Number amounts can increase (become larger) or decrease (become smaller). Using percents makes the comparison easier.

According to the newspaper headline, which company lost more workers?

NEWS

Monarch Supermarkets fires 12% of 750 employees. Ninety workers are out of a job.

NEWS

Powell Industries lets 792 of 3600 workers go — a 22% reduction.

Example

A company that had 30 workers now has only 24. What is the percent of decrease?

STEP 1 Subtract to find the amount of decrease or increase.
original − new
$30 - 24 = 6$
The amount of decrease is 6.

STEP 2 Write a percent equation and solve for n.
Remember to use n for the number you are looking for.
6 is what percent of 30?
$6 = n \times 30$
$6 = 30n$
$0.2 = n$

STEP 3 Change the decimal to a percent.
$0.2 \times 100\% = 20\%$

The percent of decrease is 20%.

ON YOUR OWN

There were 40 stores in a mall. Now there are 35. What is the percent of decrease?

Practice

Subtract to find the amount of decrease or increase. Then find the percent.

Building Skills

Find the percent of increase or decrease.

1. 60 teachers last year; 57 this year.

$$\frac{3}{60} = \frac{1}{20} = 0.05 = 5\%$$

2. Original price is 60; new price is $45.

3. Original number of seats is 800; new number of seats is 850.

4. Original number of acres is 32; new number of acres is 16.

5. Old number is 40; new number is 48.

6. Last year's score is 50; this year's score is 42.

7. Original salary is $120; new salary is $100.

8. Original price is $85; new price is $76.50.

Problem Solving

Solve.

9. Antwon used to work 50 hours each month. Now he works 45 hours a month. What is the percent of decrease?

$$50 - 45 = 5$$
$$5 = n \times 50$$
$$n = \frac{5}{50} = \frac{1}{10} = 10\%$$

10. A surfboard factory has 32 employees. As sales go up, the number of workers increases to 40. What is the percent of increase?

11. A trainee's salary is raised from $500 per week to $550 per week. What is the percent of increase?

12. A group of music stores had 300 people working for them. Now there are only 220. What is the percent of decrease?

13. The round-trip fare from New York to San Francisco was $440. It has been reduced to $396. What is the percent of decrease?

14. Last season, Jamaal's batting average was 0.240. With all his injuries this year, his average dropped to 0.192. What is the percent of decrease?

LESSON (19) Markup and Discount

To make money, stores charge you more for their items than they have to pay for them. The **markup** is the difference between what a store pays for the item and the price you pay for it.

You find the *percent of markup* the same way you find the *percent of increase*.

> markup = selling price to you − original cost to store

A **discount** is a cut in price.
You find the *percent of discount* the same way you find the *percent of decrease*.

> discount = original price − reduced price

Example

A store receives cell phones for $24 each and sells them for $36 each. What is the percent of markup?

STEP 1 Subtract to find the amount of increase or decrease.
selling price − original cost
$$36 - 24 = 12$$
The amount of increase is 12.

STEP 2 Write a percent equation and solve for n.
12 is what decimal of 24?
$$12 = n \times 24$$
$$\frac{12}{24} = \frac{24n}{24}$$
$$0.5 = n$$

STEP 3 Change the decimal to a percent.
$$0.5 \times 100\% = 50\%$$

The markup is 50%.

ON YOUR OWN

An $800 stereo system now sells for $750. What is the percent of discount?

Practice

Building Skills

Find the percent of markup or discount.

1. A store's original price for a camera is $285; the selling price is $240.

> $285 − $240 = $45
>
> $\dfrac{45}{285} = 0.1578 = 15.78\%$

2. The original price is $600; discounted price is $480.

3. The original price is $84; discounted price is $75.60.

4. The store's cost is $60; selling price is $75.

5. The store's cost is $20; selling price is $26.

6. The original price is $300; discounted price is $210.

7. The store's cost is $25; selling price is $45.

8. The store's cost is $24; selling price is $28.

Problem Solving

Solve.

9. A $75 shirt is on sale for $60. What is the percent of discount?

> $75 − 60 = 15$
>
> $\dfrac{15}{75} = 0.20 = 20\%$

10. A store paid $65 for a CD player that it sells for $80. What is the percent of markup?

11. A jacket used to sell for $160. It is now on sale for $128. What is the percent of discount?

12. A $300 suit is marked up by $120. What is the percent of markup?

13. Airfare from Miami to Phoenix usually costs $480. Now it is reduced to $410. What is the percent of discount?

14. The price for a new 32-inch television was $360. The new price is $280. What is the percent of discount?

Choose a Strategy

You can use different strategies to answer the same test question about percents. Choose the strategy that works best for you.

Example

The original price of a DVD player is $39.95. The sale price is 9% off. How much does a person save by buying the DVD on sale?

STEP 1 Think about different strategies you could use to solve the problem.
- Use compatible numbers. You could use numbers that are easy to work with first, and then use the actual numbers.
- Write an equation. You could use the percent equation: part = percent × whole.

STEP 2 Choose a strategy.
For this problem, use the *Use Compatible Numbers* strategy. Start by making the numbers in the problem easier to work with.

STEP 3 Use compatible numbers to estimate the solution.
Forty dollars is close to $39.95. Ten percent is close to 9%.
10% of $40.00 is $4. You know the answer will be about $4.

STEP 4 Now solve the problem with the actual numbers.
9% of $39.95 = .09 × 39.95 = 3.5955

A person saves $3.60 by buying the DVD on sale.

TRY IT OUT

A flower shop pays $28 for a dozen roses. The store marks the price up by 45%. How much does the store mark up the price?

Circle the correct answer.

A. $6.22   B. $9.05   C. $12.60   D. $15.40

Option C is correct. The store marks up the price by $12.60 because 45% of $28, or 0.45 × $28, is $12.60.

Overview • Lessons 20–21

Application of Percents II

Banks charge customers to borrow money. Banks also pay customers to keep money in the bank. The money banks charge or pay is called **interest**.

You can get interest on money you have in your bank account. This is **simple interest**.

5% Simple Annual Interest on $100	
End of year 1	$100 + (0.05 × $100) = $105
End of year 2	$105 + (0.05 × $100) = $110
End of Year 3	$110 + (0.05 × $100) = $115

You can get interest on the money you have in your bank account *plus* the amount of interest you have already earned. This is called **compound interest**.

5% Compound Annual Interest on $100	
End of year 1	$100 + (0.05 × $100) = $105
End of year 2	$105 + (0.05 × $105) = $110.25
End of Year 3	$110.25 + (0.05 × $110.25) = $115.76

YOU KNOW

- How to write a percent as a decimal or fraction

- How to find a percent of a number

- How to write and solve an equation to find a missing number

- The order of operations

YOU WILL LEARN

- How to find simple interest and compound interest

- How to use interest formulas

Remember the BASICS

Solve.

1. **What is 22% of $400?**
   22% = 0.22
   $n = 0.22 × 400$
   $n = 88$
   22% of $400 is $88.

2. **Find 4% of $300.**

3. **Find 2.5% of $600.**

4. $0.04 × 2500 × 3$

5. $\frac{1}{4} × 200 × 2$

6. $0.055 × 1500 × 4$

LESSON 20 Simple Interest

When you borrow money from a bank, you pay interest on the loan. When you save money in a bank, you receive interest on the money you saved.

To find simple interest, use this formula:

Interest = principal × rate × time

$$I = p \times r \times t$$

- **Interest** (*I*) is the money paid for using or saving other money.
- The **principal** (*p*) is the amount of money you start with.
- The **rate** (*r*) is the interest rate. This is the percent that the bank pays on the principal.
- The **time** (*t*) is the amount of time the money is in the bank.

Before you solve for interest, change the rate to a decimal and be sure the time is in years.

Example

How much simple interest will you earn when you put $600 in your bank at 4% interest for 6 months? How much money will be in this account at the end of 6 months?

STEP 1 Use the simple interest formula.
$$I = p \times r \times t$$
Substitute the numbers for the letters.
$$I = p \times r \times t$$
$$I = \$600 \times 4\% \times 6 \text{ months}$$

STEP 2 Multiply to find the *simple interest*.
Change percents to decimals. Change months to years.
$$I = \$600 \times 0.04 \times 0.5$$
$$I = \$12$$
You will earn $12 in simple interest.

STEP 3 Add to find the *total amount*.
$$\$600 + \$12 = \$612$$
$$\downarrow \qquad \downarrow \qquad \downarrow$$
Principal Interest Total amount

You will have $612 in your account after 6 months.

ON YOUR OWN

You save $3,000 for 2 years in a bank that has an interest rate of 5% per year. Find the interest. Find the total amount in your account after 2 years.

Practice

Write the rate as a decimal before you multiply.

Building Skills

Find the simple interest only.

1. $800 deposited at 3% for 2 years

$I = p \times r \times t$
$I = \$800 \times 0.03 \times 2 = \$48$
The simple interest on $800 at 3% for 2 years is $48.

2. $4,000 deposited at 4% for 1 year

3. $500 deposited at 5% for 2 years

4. $700 deposited at 3.5% for 0.5 year

Find the simple interest and total amount.

5. $1,000 deposited at 8% for 2 years

6. $900 deposited at 7.5% for 5 years

7. $1,300 deposited at 5.4% for 1 year

8. $800 deposited at 9% for 9 months

Problem Solving

Solve.

9. What will the total amount be after 3 years for a savings deposit of $320 at 6% interest?

$I = p \times r \times t$
$I = 320 \times 0.06 \times 3 = 57.60$
$320.00 + 57.60 = 377.60$

10. A deposit is made of $900 at 5% interest for 6 months. How much interest will be earned during that time?

11. You deposit $1,100 for 9 months at 9% interest. How much interest will be earned during that time? How much money will be in the account at the end of this time?

12. Elena deposits $240 at 6% interest for $1\frac{1}{2}$ years. How much interest will be in her account at the end of that time?

13. You have $450 to put in a savings account. In 9 months, how much more will you have at $8\frac{1}{2}$% interest than at 8% interest? (Hint: You are finding the difference between two rates.)

14. Ming saved $1,000 at $6\frac{3}{4}$% for $2\frac{1}{2}$ years. How much money will be in his account at the end of $2\frac{1}{2}$ years?

LESSON ㉑ Compound Interest

You have learned that simple interest is paid only on the principal (the amount of money you start with). **Compound interest** is paid on the principal plus *any interest* that has built up in your account.

In other words, the interest you earn or pay gets interest too.

You can use the following formula to find the balance in an account that earns compound interest.

$$B = p(1 + r)^t$$

(**B**) **balance** of an account is the principal plus any interest earned.

p is principal.
r is rate of interest.
t is time.

> **Order of Operations**
> **P**arentheses
> **E**xponents
> **M**ultiplication or
> **D**ivision
> **A**ddition or
> **S**ubtraction

Example

You put $3,000 in a savings account that pays 4% interest compounded annually (each year). What is your balance after three years?

STEP 1 Write the formula for compound interest.

$$B = p(1 + r)^t$$

STEP 2 Substitute numbers into the formula. Change the interest rate (*r*) to a decimal.

$$B = p(1 + r)^t$$
$$B = 3,000(1 + 0.04)^3$$

STEP 3 Solve using the order of operations.
$$B = 3,000(1.04)^3$$
$$B = 3,000(1.124864)$$
$$B = 3,374.592$$

STEP 4 Round your answer to the nearest cent.

The balance in your account after 3 years is $3,374.59.

ON YOUR OWN

You put $400 in the bank for 4 years at a rate of 5% compounded annually. Find the total amount in your account after four years.

Practice

An exponent tells you how many times to multiply a number by itself.

Building Skills

Find the balance in each account using the compound interest formula.

1. $600 deposited at 4% after 2 years

$$B = p(1 + r)^t$$
$$B = 600(1 + 0.04)^2$$
$$B = 600(1.04)^2$$
$$= \$648.96$$

2. $900 deposited at 6% after 3 years

3. $900 deposited at 4% after 5 years

4. $1,800 deposited at 6% after 4 years

5. $2,000 deposited at 4.5% after 1 year

6. $3,000 deposited at 4.25% after 12 years

7. $5,000 deposited at 4% after 5 years

8. $4,250 deposited at 6% after 4 years

Problem Solving

Solve.

9. Marshall put $500 in an account paying 8% compounded annually. How much was the account worth after 15 years?

$$B = p(1 + r)^t$$
$$B = 500(1 + 0.08)^{15}$$
$$B = 500(1.08)^{15}$$
$$= 1,586.08$$

10. A deposit of $300 earns 4% interest for 3 years compounded *quarterly* (every 3 months or 0.25 of a year). What will the total amount in this account be after three years?

11. You deposit $1,000 at 10% compounded annually. What is your balance after a year and a half?

12. $9,000 is deposited in a savings account. The money is left there for two years. It earns 6% interest compounded semiannually (twice a year). How much money will be in the account after two years? (*Hint: r* = 0.03, *t* = 4.)

13. Joshua's great-grandfather deposited $1,000 in an account that earns 5% interest compounded annually. The money stayed there for 100 years. What was the account worth at the end of 100 years?

14. An account pays 6% compounded monthly. What is the value of $150 left in the account for 1 year?

TEST-TAKING STRATEGY

Make a Table

You can make a table to help you answer test questions about interest.

Example

A bank pays 1.5% interest compounded annually on savings accounts. Mr. Chen opened a savings account with $5,000. If he does not take out any money, in how many years will he have more than $5,300?

STEP 1 Find the balance for the end of the first year.

Find the interest for one year. $\rightarrow$ $I = p \times r \times t$
$$I = 5,000 \times 0.015 \times 1$$
$$I = 75 \times 1$$
$$I = 75$$

Add the interest to the principal. $\rightarrow$ $5,000 + 75 = 5,075$

The balance at the end of the first year will be $5,075.

STEP 2 Make a table that shows the principal at the beginning of each year, the interest paid, and the balance at the end of each year.
Round each amount to the nearest dollar.

Year	Principal	Interest	Ending Balance
1	$5,000	× 0.015 × 1 = $75	$5,075
2	$5,075	× 0.015 × 1 = $76	$5,151
3	$5,151	× 0.015 × 1 = $77	$5,228
4	$5,228	× 0.015 × 1 = $78	$5,306

Mr. Chen's account balance will exceed $5,300 in 4 years.

TRY IT OUT

Maria opened a savings account that pays 1.3% interest compounded annually. She deposited $2,500 in the account. If she does not take out any money from the account, how many years will it take for the balance to go above $2,700?

Circle the correct answer.

A. 4 years   B. 5 years   C. 6 years   D. 7 years

Option C is correct. The account balance will be $2,702 at the end of the sixth year.

Find the percent of increase or decrease.

1. Old number is 30; new number is 15

2. Old number is 15; new number is 30

Find the percent of markup.

3. Store's cost is $40; selling price is $55

4. Store's cost is $200; selling price is $225

Find the percent of discount.

5. Original price is $600; discounted price is $480

6. Original price is $240; discounted price is $204

Find the simple interest.

7. $400 deposited for 3 years at 4.5% simple interest

8. $1,200 deposited for half a year at 6% simple interest

Find the simple interest and the total balance.

9. $200 deposited at 6% for 1 year

10. $2,500 deposited at 4.5% for 3 years

Use compound interest to find the balance.

11. Principal is $200; rate is 6%; compounded annually for 4 years

12. Principal is $500; rate is 5%; compounded annually for 3 years

Solve.

13. Jackson's salary was raised from $800 a week to $850. By what percent was his salary increased?

14. The price of a sweater is lowered from $60 to $44. What percent is the discount?

15. Bill took out a loan for $500. The loan is for 3 years at 5% simple interest. How much will Bill pay back?

16. A new father put $600 into an account for his child's sixteenth birthday. The money earns 6% interest compounded semiannually (twice a year). How much money will be in the account after 2 years?

Post Test

Take this Post Test after you have completed this book. The Post Test will help you determine how far you have progressed in building your math skills.

Use the list of numbers to the right to answer questions 1 and 2.

$$2 \quad 9 \quad 11 \quad 12 \quad 16 \quad 23 \quad 33$$

1. What is the ratio of even numbers to odd numbers? _____

2. What is the ratio of odd numbers to all the numbers? _____

Write each rate in simplest form.

3. 120 words in 2 minutes

4. 60 miles on 3 gallons of gas

Solve.

5. Leticia bought 6 bottles of water for $2.40. What is the price per bottle?

6. A 6-pound watermelon sells for $1.95. What is the price per pound?

Write = or ≠ in the box.

7. $\dfrac{5}{8} \ \square \ \dfrac{16}{10}$

8. $\dfrac{4}{7} \ \square \ \dfrac{12}{21}$

Solve for *n*.

9. $\dfrac{4}{n} = \dfrac{12}{3}$

10. $\dfrac{n}{8} = \dfrac{48}{16}$

Solve.

11. Two out of every 7 players in the league were chosen for the all-star teams. There are 224 players. How many were chosen?

12. Ariel is paid by the hour. During one week, she worked 24 hours and earned $336. What is Ariel's hourly pay?

Write each decimal or fraction as a percent.

13. $\dfrac{5}{16}$

14. 0.062

Write each percent as a fraction in simplest form.

15. 42%

16. 115%

Solve.

17. Find 40% of 62.

18. What percent of 60 is 24?

19. 1.4 is 20% percent of what number?

20. 17 is what percent of 68?

21. You purchase 25% of a stamp collection. You bought 18 stamps. How many stamps were in the whole collection?

22. All products in a salon go on sale for 10% off next week. Today, a hair conditioner sells for $21. How much less will that same product cost next week?

Find the interest.

23. $1,200 deposited for 3 years at an annual rate of 5% simple interest

24. $400 deposited for 6 months at 4.5% simple interest

Find the balance in the account.

25. Principal is $100; compound interest rate is 7.5% compounded annually; time is 2 years

Glossary

balance (*B*) (page 68)
the principal plus any interest earned

compound interest (page 68)
the money paid based on the principal plus the interest already earned; the formula for finding the balance on an account that earns compound interest is
$B = p(1 + r)^n$

cross multiply (page 16)
to multiply the numerator of one ratio by the denominator of the other ratio in a proportion

cross products (page 16)
the answer to multiplying the numerator of one ratio by the denominator of the other ratio in a proportion

denominator
the number below the fraction bar in a fraction

discount (page 62)
a cut in price

equation
a statement of equality between two terms

equivalent (page 16)
when two things are equal

equivalent fractions (page 7)
fractions that name the same amount

equivalent ratios (page 16)
fractions written as equivalent fractions

exponent (page 68)
a number that tells how many times a number, or base, is used as a factor

formula
a rule that shows the relationship between two or more quantities; for example, the formula for calculating simple interest is
$I = prt$

greatest common factor (**GCF**) (page 7)
the greatest number that is a factor of two or more numbers; for example, the greatest common factor of 18 and 30 is 6

interest (*I*) (page 66)
the money paid for using or saving other money; the amount banks charge or pay on money borrowed or saved

interest rate (page 66)
the rate, given as a percent, used to determine interest; the percent a bank pays or charges on the principal

markup (page 62)
the difference between what a store pays for an item and its selling price

numerator
number above the fraction bar in a fraction

percent (page 30)
a special ratio that compares a number to 100; another way of saying *per hundred*

percent equation (page 52)
an equation used to show and solve percent problems

percent of change (increase or decrease) (page 60)
the percent a quantity increases or decreases from its original amount

principal (*p*) (page 66)
the amount of money you start with, for example, the original amount of a loan

proportion (page 16)
a statement that says two ratios are equal

proportional reasoning
using proportions as a way to reason and solve everyday problems

rate (*r*) (page 10)
a ratio that compares two quantities (amounts) measured in different units; also, the percent of interest paid on the principal

ratio (page 8)
compares two quantities, amounts, or numbers. Ratios must be written in simplest form.

simple interest (page 66)
money paid based only on the principal ($I = prt$)

simplest form (page 8)
a fraction in which the numerator and denominator have no common factors other than 1

term (page 22)
the name given to each value in a proportion

time (*t*) (page 66)
the amount of time money is in the bank

unit price (page 12)
the unit rate that tells the price per unit; the cost of one item

unit rate (page 12)
the rate for one unit of a quantity. The denominator for any unit rate is 1.

variable (page 52)
a letter used to represent the number you are trying to find

Math Toolkit

Key Operation Words

Word problems often contain clues that help you solve the problem. These words tell you whether you need to add, subtract, multiply, or divide. The lists of words below will help you decide which operation to use when solving word problems.

Addition
add
all together
and
both
combined
in all
increase
more
plus
sum
total

Subtraction
change (money)
decrease
difference
left
less than
more than
reduce
remain or remaining
smaller, larger, farther, nearer, and so on

Multiplication
in all
of
multiply
product
times (as much)
total
twice
whole

Division
average
cut
divide
each
equal pieces
every
one
split

Percent Triangle

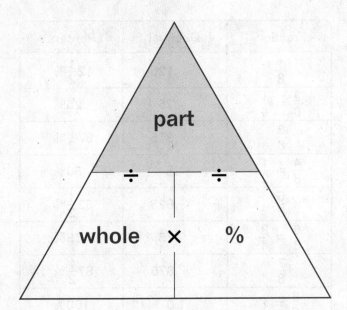

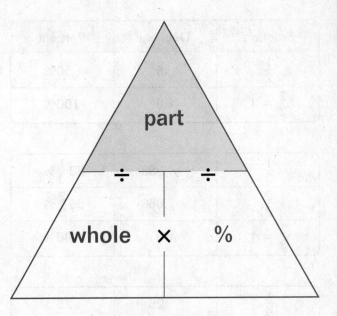

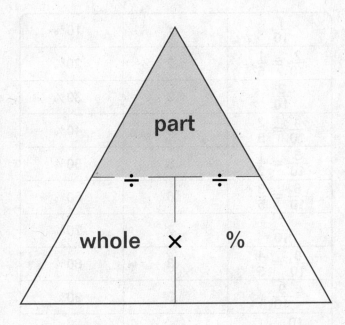

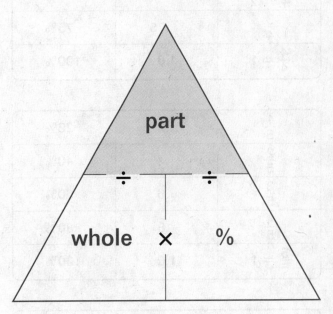

Math Toolkit

Equivalent Fractions, Decimals, and Percents

Fraction	Decimal	Percent
$\frac{1}{2}$	.5	50%
$\frac{2}{2} = 1$	1.0	100%

Fraction	Decimal	Percent
$\frac{1}{3}$	$.33\overline{3}$	$33\frac{1}{3}\%$
$\frac{2}{3}$	$.66\overline{6}$	$66\frac{2}{3}\%$
$\frac{3}{3} = 1$	1.0	100%

Fraction	Decimal	Percent
$\frac{1}{4}$	.25	25%
$\frac{2}{4} = \frac{1}{2}$	.5	50%
$\frac{3}{4}$	.75	75%
$\frac{4}{4} = 1$	1.0	100%

Fraction	Decimal	Percent
$\frac{1}{5}$	.2	20%
$\frac{2}{5}$	.4	40%
$\frac{3}{5}$	.6	60%
$\frac{4}{5}$	.8	80%
$\frac{5}{5} = 1$	1.0	100%

Fraction	Decimal	Percent
$\frac{1}{6}$	$.16\overline{6}$	$16\frac{2}{3}\%$
$\frac{2}{6} = \frac{1}{3}$	$.33\overline{3}$	$33\frac{1}{3}\%$
$\frac{3}{6} = \frac{1}{2}$	.5	50%
$\frac{4}{6} = \frac{2}{3}$	$.66\overline{6}$	$66\frac{2}{3}\%$
$\frac{5}{6}$	$.83\overline{3}$	$83\frac{1}{3}\%$
$\frac{6}{6} = 1$	1.0	100%

Fraction	Decimal	Percent
$\frac{1}{8}$	.125	$12\frac{1}{2}\%$
$\frac{2}{8} = \frac{1}{4}$	.25	25%
$\frac{3}{8}$	.375	$37\frac{1}{2}\%$
$\frac{4}{8} = \frac{1}{2}$	.5	50%
$\frac{5}{8}$	.625	$62\frac{1}{2}\%$
$\frac{6}{8} = \frac{3}{4}$	.75	75%
$\frac{7}{8}$	.875	$87\frac{1}{2}\%$
$\frac{8}{8} = 1$	1.0	100%

Fraction	Decimal	Percent
$\frac{1}{10}$	.1	10%
$\frac{2}{10} = \frac{1}{5}$	.2	20%
$\frac{3}{10}$	.3	30%
$\frac{4}{10} = \frac{2}{5}$	.4	40%
$\frac{5}{10} = \frac{1}{2}$	.5	50%
$\frac{6}{10} = \frac{3}{5}$	.6	60%
$\frac{7}{10}$	.7	70%
$\frac{8}{10} = \frac{4}{5}$	.8	80%
$\frac{9}{10}$	.9	90%
$\frac{10}{10} = 1$	1.0	100%

Fraction	Decimal	Percent
$\frac{1}{100}$	.01	1%
1	1.0	100%